Mitch on a Ranch

by Rhonda Martin
illustrated by Meryl Henderson

Core Decodable 42

McGraw Hill Education

Bothell, WA • Chicago, IL • Columbus, OH • New York, NY

MHEonline.com

Send all inquiries to:
McGraw-Hill Education
8787 Orion Place
Columbus, OH 43240

ISBN: 978-0-02-145734-2
MHID: 0-02-145734-4

Printed in Canada.

9 10 11 12 KOD 24

This is Mitch.

Mitch is on a ranch.

Mitch helps Dad hitch up the truck.

Mitch checks on the chicks.
This chick just hatched.

Dad's truck is stuck in a ditch!

Mitch fetches Patch.

Patch catches on and helps.
The truck is not in the ditch.

Dad pats Patch.
Mitch gets Patch a snack.